The British Passport Interview:
A concise guide

Published by Garuda Publications and available from:
Garuda Publications
41 Beech Close
Walton-on-Thames
Surrey KT12 5RQ, UK

Email: Sales@GarudaPublications.com
www.GarudaPublications.com

Written and edited by Andrew Thompson

ISBN 978-0-9565738-6-5

Contents

Introduction

What happens at the British Passport interview? What questions are asked?

This guide provides information about the interview that all adults applying for the first time for a British Passport are asked to undergo. The guide has pulled together in one place what is known about the interview. Examples of the types of questions that applicants are likely to be asked at interview are included.

Having read this guide passport applicants should understand the British Passport Interview process and have a good idea of the types of questions that they will be asked during the interview itself.

For most the interview for a British passport proves a straightforward and simple experience. We hope that this guide makes the process less daunting.

Who is this guide for?

This guide is for adults who have successfully applied for British Citizenship and been given their naturalisation certificate.

One of the surprises for those who have successfully applied for British Citizenship and attended a Citizenship Ceremony is that they aren't automatically given a British passport at the end of the process. At the citizenship ceremony new British citizens are presented with their Naturalisation Certificate.

Instead, the 'Being a British Citizen' information pack which new citizens are given during the course of the British Citizenship ceremony contains an application form for a British passport. If you lose the form you can get one at a Post Office.

You must have British nationality to be eligible for a British passport. So, armed with British Nationality, in the form of the Naturalisation

Certificate, new citizens become eligible for a British passport and can begin the application process.

The next thing that many new citizens discover for the first time is that they will have to attend an interview before they can receive their passport.

Who is interviewed?

HM Passport Office is the sole issuer of UK passports. They are part of the Home Office. This is what they say about who will be interviewed:

> *"If you are 16 or over, or likely to become 16 before we can issue your passport, you may need to have an identity interview."*

In practice this means that 99.9% of all citizens who have become British through naturalisation are interviewed.

You may not need an interview if you were born on or before 2 September 1929.

Why are people interviewed?

The purpose of the interview is to help the Home Office improve passport security and protect the applicant from having their identity stolen.

HM Passport Office say:

> *"The interview will help us to confirm your identity and that the passport application we have checked actually belongs to you. This is an important part of our commitment to help to reduce identity fraud. It will help us to spot and prevent other people using your identity and committing fraud in your name."*

Although not many people's applications are rejected as a result of the requirement to attend an 'identity interview' the interview is regarded as a deterrent to those seeking a real British passport with a false identity.

For many applicants this may well be the first time that they have been seen in person by a representative of the UK government since first applying to come to the UK with a visa several years previously.

What triggers the interview?

The act of applying for a British passport triggers the interview process. Nothing happens until you submit an application form for a British passport.

HM Passport Office state:

"You should send us your application form in the normal way. We will then write to tell you how to make an appointment for an identity interview.

This process will increase the time it takes for us to process your application. You should allow at least six weeks for your passport to be issued."

The British passport application process

Since the British passport form contains a lot of the information that you are likely to be asked about during the interview it is worth saying a little bit about it.

The most obvious advice is to '*keep a copy of whatever is submitted*' as a reminder of the information you supplied.

For example, the form may include the date that your parents got married. This is not a date that many applicants would normally know but is one of the questions regularly asked during the interview - 'When did your parents get married?'

In terms of the practicalities of applying for a British passport, you can:

Fill in your information online (*www.gov.uk/apply-renew-passport*) then print and post your form, photos and documents to the address on the form (you can't use the Passport Check and Send service if you fill in the form online); or

Get a paper form from a Post Office that offers the Passport Check and Send service; or contact the Passport Advice line and get a form posted to you

> Telephone: 0300 222 0000
> Textphone: 0300 222 0222
> Text Relay: 18001 0300 222 0000

Monday to Friday, 8am to 8pm
Saturday, Sunday and public holidays, 9am to 5:30pm

How long does the whole process take?

It takes *'at least 6 weeks'* to get your first UK adult passport. HM Passport office advise applicants not to book travel until they have received the passport.

Making the passport interview appointment

After you apply for a British Passport, if you are to be called for an interview you will be sent a letter asking you to attend an interview to confirm your identity.

The letter from HM Passport Office will ask you to phone for an appointment at a passport interview office.

Appointments are made by calling the telephone number supplied in the letter. Applicants have to quote the unique reference number at the top of the letter.

Typically the letter includes a list of the interview offices together with their opening times.

If you go to *www.gov.uk/passport-interview-office* and input your postcode the online service will bring up a list of the nearest offices where interviews are held.

The most recently published list (*www.gov.uk/government/ publications/list-of-interview-offices*) identifies 35 offices across the UK where interviews are conducted [published 5 February 2011, most likely in response to a Freedom of Information Act request].

You can choose the office you go to, but you may not get the exact time or date you want. Many of the offices operate on a part time basis. The booking line advisors will be able to confirm the days and times that it is possible to attend.

The passport interview offices are for interviews only – they can't give you a passport there and then.

HM Passport Office may be able to arrange an interview closer to you if you live in a remote area. Ask when you phone.

Customers who live in remote postcode areas may be entitled to the option of interview via video link. If eligible they will be offered a list of additional locations.

The interview confirmation notification

Once the passport interview is booked applicants receive confirmation. Typically this is in the form of an email confirmation.

The correspondence will confirm the date, location and time of the appointment and usually provide a map and directions.

Applicants are asked to arrive 10 minutes before the interview appointment and to let the office know of any particular needs in advance of the interview.

The letter states that the interview process will usually take about 30 minutes to complete.

Applicants are warned that if they fail to turn up for a booked interview without giving at least 24 hours' notice HM Passport Office may withdraw their passport application.

So, if you don't turn up for the interview you may have to start the whole passport application process again.

What to take to the interview?

You do not need to bring any documents to the interview. However, you should bring your appointment invitation or confirmation letter as it will have your unique reference number on it.

Attending the interview

On the day make sure you arrive early so that you are not late because of any last minute difficulties finding the office where the interview is to be conducted. The interviews are often held in grey faceless impersonal buildings and it is not always as easy to find the correct location as you might think.

The interview office is happy for you to arrive 10 minutes before the appointment. However, if you arrive before this time they can, and do, ask you to leave and return at your scheduled time.

If you arrive late and miss your appointment there is no guarantee that you will be seen that day.

A relative, friend or representative may come with you to the interview office, but they will not be allowed to sit in on your interview (unless this has been agreed beforehand).

Applicants are discouraged from bringing children to the interview offices.

What happens when you arrive?

When you arrive at reception a member of staff will check that you look like the photograph you included with your British passport application.

You will also be asked to confirm some basic information given on your application form such as your full address.

The address information you give needs to match the information on the application form.

In the unlikely event that the office cannot identify you from the photograph you included with your application or your answers do not match the information given on your application form then you will not be interviewed that day

In these very rare instances the staff will tell you what to do before booking another appointment.

Having passed these initial checks the candidate is invited into a room for the formal interview process.

The interview itself

Interviews are conducted by a civil servant, trained to conduct interviews for HM Passport Service. There is usually only the candidate and the interviewer in the interview room. The rooms used for the interviews are fairly standard offices.

The interviewer will have a PC on which he can pull up details of the applicant. A camera is also visible on the desk as all of the interviews are recorded.

Interview recordings are for quality and review purposes and to help HM Passport Office to make a fair decision. They may be used for training purposes. Recordings are destroyed after passports are issued.

The interviewer will say hello and ask the applicant to take a seat before commencing
the interview.

You are NOT ALLOWED to take ANY papers or ANY Electronic devices into the interview room with you.

Those reporting on the interview experience generally describe them as 'friendly but thorough'.

All interviews are conducted IN ENGLISH. Given that applicants will usually have passed The Life in the UK Test and other English Language qualifications as part of their successful British Citizenship application no translator support is permitted.

What will I be asked?

Perhaps unsurprisingly HM Passport office does not provide any examples of the types of questions that will be asked during the interview. However, through dialogue with those who have been through the interviews, the official guidance and by distilling down what individuals have posted on the internet and social media it is possible to work out many aspects of the interview.

It is worth considering what HM Passport office says it will ask applicants in the guidance notes for passport applications:

"We will ask you to confirm basic information about yourself, including information that someone trying to steal your identity

may not know. Our questions will be based on information you give in your application form and from our searches of public and private-sector databases, including credit-reference agencies. The questions we ask will not be the same at every interview."

On the *www.gov.uk* website it simply says:

"You'll be asked questions about yourself to make sure you are who you claim to be."

When the passport interviews were first launched the government of the day also said that:

"Applicants will be asked about their ancestry, including the background of their parents, previous addresses, details about counter-signatories and other questions designed to establish a 'social footprint" of who they are."

Before moving on to consider the types of questions that come up it is worth thinking about what HM Passport office will know about you as an applicant.

Information that you have supplied them with directly:

- They have your application form

- They have any information submitted with your application

- They will know how you applied

- They will be able to access your complete visa application history

For example, if you look at the passport application form you can see that you supply a lot of information. You can expect to be asked questions to confirm any of the information on the form.

The passport application form captures the information below:

Your details

- Your name

- Maiden or all previous names

- Address

- Country of birth

- Date of birth

- Town of birth

- Mobile Number

- Alternative number

- Email address

- Details of any previous passport – British or otherwise

- Details of any lost or stolen passport

Parents' details

Mother's or Parent 1's full name

- Date of their birth

- Their nationality at time of the applicant's birth

- Whether they have a British passport

- Date of issue

- Their date of marriage or civil partnership to the father or second parent

Father's or Parent 2's full name

- Town and country of birth

- Date of birth

- Nationality and citizenship at the time of the applicants birth

- Whether they have British passport

- Date of issue

Certificate or registration or naturalisation

- Whether the applicant has been granted a certificate of registration or naturalization

- Certificate number

- Place of issue

- Date of issue

Countersignature

- Name of countersignature

- Address of countersignature

- Number of years that countersignature has known applicant

- How the countersignature has known the applicant – employer, colleague, friend

- Confirmation that British signature holds a valid UK or Irish passport

- Profession, professional qualifications or position in the community of the counter signature

- The employer's address for the countersignature
  (or private address, as relevant)

- The passport number of the countersignature

- The contact telephone numbers for the countersignature

Signatures

- The signature of the applicant

- The signature of the countersignatures

Information that they have been able to source:

HM Passport Office does not reveal what level of information they source or who supplies it but we know that they will have:

- Credit reference information

- Court and insolvency information

- Information from the electoral roll

Similar information is sourced as part of the checks when considering applications for British citizenship so it is logical that this kind of information will also be available for the passport interview.

How many questions will I be asked?

Back in 2007 the Daily Telegraph reported that there was a pool of some 200 questions from which those to be asked at the interview would be drawn.

The actual number of questions people report as having been asked does vary but the typical reported range seems to be between 20 and 30 questions.

Example questions

The questions below are examples of the types of questions that are likely to be asked. HM Passport Office does not publish any information on the actual questions.

During the interview, do not be surprised if you are asked for the same information but in a slightly different way. There are likely to be some 'cross-check questions'. These will be straightforward for the honest candidate but are likely to present difficulties to someone attempting to mislead the interviewer.

For example, you might be asked "How many people live with you?" and later in the interview "Who do you live with?"

'Meet and greet questions':

- How did you get here today? (what route - bus/train, etc)

- How long did it take you to get here?

- How will you get home?

Questions related to the information you have supplied directly:

- Your full name? [you will be asked to spell this]

- Please sign your name on the 'electronic pad' [signature check]

- Where do you live?

- What's your address? [note - the full address and postcode must match the application form]

- Parents name?

- Parents date of birth?

- Mother's maiden name?

- When did your parents get married?

- Where were your parents born?

- Where were you born?

- Have you been known by any other names?

- What was your previous address?

- What papers did you send with your application?

- How did you send your passport application? [For example, check and send at a Post Office]

- Did you get the papers back?

- Date of your naturalization certificate?

- When did you take the UK citizenship ceremony?

- Where was your UK citizenship ceremony taken?

- What did they give you at the UK citizenship ceremony?

- Your date of birth?

- Your marital status?

- When did you get married? [if relevant]

- Where did you get married? [if relevant]

- Partner's name? [if relevant]

- Partner's date of birth? [if relevant]

- Partner's occupation?

- Your occupation?

- Children's name(s) [if relevant]

- Children's date(s) of birth? [if relevant]

- What name shall we send the passport to?

- What is your telephone number?

- What is your email address?

- Who counter-signed your passport picture on the application form?

- What is the occupation of the person who countersigned your application?

- How long have you known the person who counter-signed your application picture?

- When and where did you take The Life in the UK Test?

- What was your route to British Citizenship?

Questions related to information that HM Passport Office has sourced independently:

- Do you have a mortgage?

- Who is the mortgage with?

- Who do you bank with?

- How many people live with you?

- Does anyone else over the age of 16 live in your house? [who?]

- Who do you live with?

- What type of house do you have? (detached, semi-detached, terraced)

- How many bedrooms does your house have?

- How long have you lived at your current address?

- Where did you live before?

- Do you have a garden? (front/back/both)

- Where do your children go to school?

- What's your landlord/estate agent name? (if renting)

- How many bank accounts you have?

- How many credit cards you have?

- Do you have any loans? [with whom]

- Do you have any mobile phone contracts? [with whom]

- Which credit and store cards do you hold?

- Who is your Broadband/Telephone/Gas/Electricity Provider?

- Do you drive a vehicle?

- What is the make and registration number of your family car?

- Where do you work?

- How do you get to work?

- How long does it take you to get to work?

- How do you get paid?

- Which supermarket do you shop at? (How do you get there?)

- What is your National Insurance Number?

- Are there any places of interest near where you live or work?

After the interview

The interviewer will not tell you at the interview if your application is successful.

HM Passport Office state:

> "We will need to carry out some final checks before we can make a decision."

What happens if I got some questions wrong?

There are two scenarios here. If you don't get the screening questions correct when you talk with reception at the start of the process – for example by not being able to give the correct address information then you may well not even be interviewed and will have to start the passport application process again.

In terms of the actual interview the consensus on the various forums and social   media where people have posted about their interview experience is that it is OK not to be able to answer some of the questions. What is not smart is to 'guess' and give incorrect answers.

It is important to remember that the purpose of the interview is to check your identity. Any attempt to mislead or deceive the interviewer could lead to problems with the application. It is far better to simply state that you cannot remember or are unsure of a particular date or fact. Hopefully that will not be true for all the questions you are asked!

In most cases the interviews are conducted by experienced interviewers who will have seen many applicants. They have been trained to pick up deception. It is far better to be truthful at interview.

How long will it take for my passport to arrive?

Passports may arrive within 2 weeks of the passport interview. All of the forums and social media state that it is usually quite a fast turn-around after the interview.

HM Passport Office says that applicants should allow at least a 6 week time-frame for the whole process from submission of application to passport issue. In our experience this is a fair estimate.

How will my passport be delivered?

In most cases, your passport will be delivered by courier (on behalf of HM Passport Office between 8am and 6pm, Monday to Saturday. In areas where there's a low risk of deliveries being lost, your passport may be delivered by Royal Mail Recorded Delivery.

In most cases the courier will not need you to sign for your passport. Couriers use technology that records the address, time and date of the delivery, and the courier will take a photo of the property where the passport was delivered

The courier will not post your passport in an outside letterbox. They will leave a calling card for you to arrange delivery at a convenient date. The secure delivery company does not recognise any mail redirection arrangements that you may have made with Royal Mail.

If your passport is being delivered by Royal Mail you will need to sign for it. If you're not at home, they will leave a calling card explaining how to rearrange delivery or collect from your local sorting office. You should do so quickly, as your passport will be returned to HM Passport Office after seven days.

Conclusion

While it is frustrating for many who have just gone through the process of gaining British Citizenship to then have to attend an interview for a British passport most applicants report the process as having been relatively painless. The interview process is generally regarded as friendly, fair and thorough. Most applicants receive their passports very shortly after the interview.

It is worth reviewing the information supplied on the form and thinking about what you are likely to be asked. Do make sure that your address information is correct. Beyond this common sense preparation there is no need for further study.

Good luck with your interview!

References and further information

Information on applying for your first adult passport is found at:
www.gov.uk/apply-first-adult-passport/your-passport-interview

The guidance material that is supplied together with the application form for a British Passport contains information about the interview for a British passport:
www.gov.uk/government/uploads/system/uploads/attachment_data/ file/476009/Applying_for_your_passport.pdf

The location of the offices that conduct passport interviews can be searched for by postcode here:
www.gov.uk/passport-interview-office

Passport application fees and how to pay are found here:
https://www.gov.uk/apply-first-adult-passport/fees-and-how-to-pay

HM Passport Office is the sole issuer of UK passports and responsible for civil registration services through the General Register Office. They are part of the Home Office.

The HM Passport Office website is found here:
www.gov.uk/government/organisations/hm-passport-office

The Life in the UK Test Handbook:

Essential independent study guide on the test for 'Settlement in the UK' and 'British Citizenship', 3rd edition

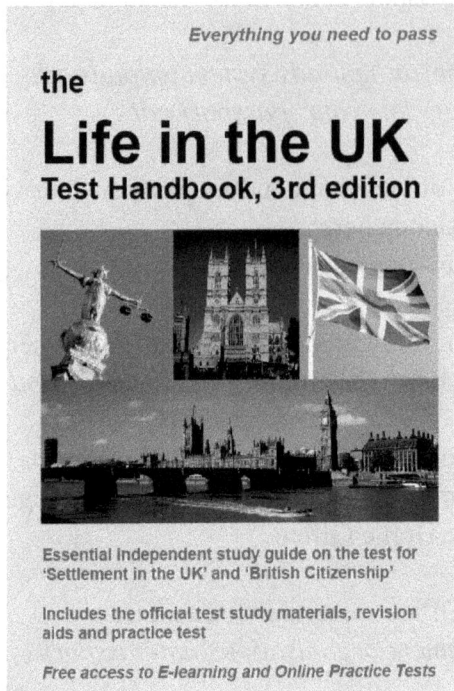

Everything you need to pass

the

Life in the UK
Test Handbook, 3rd edition

Essential independent study guide on the test for 'Settlement in the UK' and 'British Citizenship'

Includes the official test study materials, revision aids and practice test

Free access to E-learning and Online Practice Tests

'Contains everything you'll need to pass the test'

- The official study material for the test from '*Life in the United Kingdom: A guide for new residents, 3rd edition*'
- 'Statements that are True' to help you revise
- A full practice test
- Glossary of essential words and phrases
- Listing of all people mentioned in the study material
- Checklist of the conflicts mentioned in the study material
- Table of all the battles mentioned in the study material
- A list of key documents and legislation in the guidance
- Diary checklist showing the annual calendar events; and
- An historic UK timeline
- Colour illustrations and diagrams throughout